We often hear of the famous Knights of the Round Table in books, movie adaptations, and bedtime stories about King Arthur and his knights. Part of the Arthurian tale is the most enduring legend of all-the quest for the Holy Grail.

What is the Holy Grail?

The Holy Grail is a miraculous object or vessel of some sort, like a chalice. It is believed to have been used as a cup during Christ's Last Supper, the night before he was crucified.

Sir Galahad's Quest and Other Tales of the Knights of the Round Table

Children's Arthurian Folk Tales

BABY PROFESSOR

EDUCATION KIDS

Speedy Publishing LLC

40 E. Main St. #1156

Newark, DE 19711

www.speedypublishing.com

Copyright 2016

Some say that the Grail has powers which provide happiness, eternal youth, and infinite food resources in abundant supply. The search for this object was the prime quest of the Knights of King Arthur. One of these gallant knights was Galahad, the son of Sir Lancelot.

In the course of such pursuit one day, a group of knights found a sword in a stone by a river. It was said that the sword could only be pulled out by the world's best knight.

Surprisingly, Sir Galahad was able to draw the sword out and, thus, earned the right to be chosen as one of the three knights to undertake the quest of finding the Holy Grail.

Galahad had always been known as the "Perfect Knight." He was "perfect" in courage, gentleness, courtesy, and chivalry. Sir Galahad's adventure was similar to that of King Arthur, where the young Arthur managed to pull out Excalibur, the mighty sword, from a stone.

Arthur then became king

King Arthur and his knights were basically looked up to as role models of goodness. They fought against evil and brought justice to the land.

In pursuit of their quest for the Holy Grail, there were adventures of some of the knights--- Sir Percivale and Sir Gawaine. The Adventure of Sir Percivale. Sir Percivale badly wanted to find Galahad in order to overcome him for his own greater glory.

Percival sought guidance from an old recluse about Galahad's whereabouts. His aunt told him the way. Percivale proceeded to find Galahad but was attacked by twenty knights. They killed his horse. Luckily, Galahad came to his rescue and saved Percivale's life. Percivale did not know it was Galahad.

Sir Galahad simply rode away again, still insisting on pursuing the quest for the Holy Grail alone. Then a lady appeared before Percivale, gave him a black horse. The horse ran wild for four days' journey in just an hour. It was about to plunge into the sea when Percival crossed himself in fright and broke the horse's demonic power.

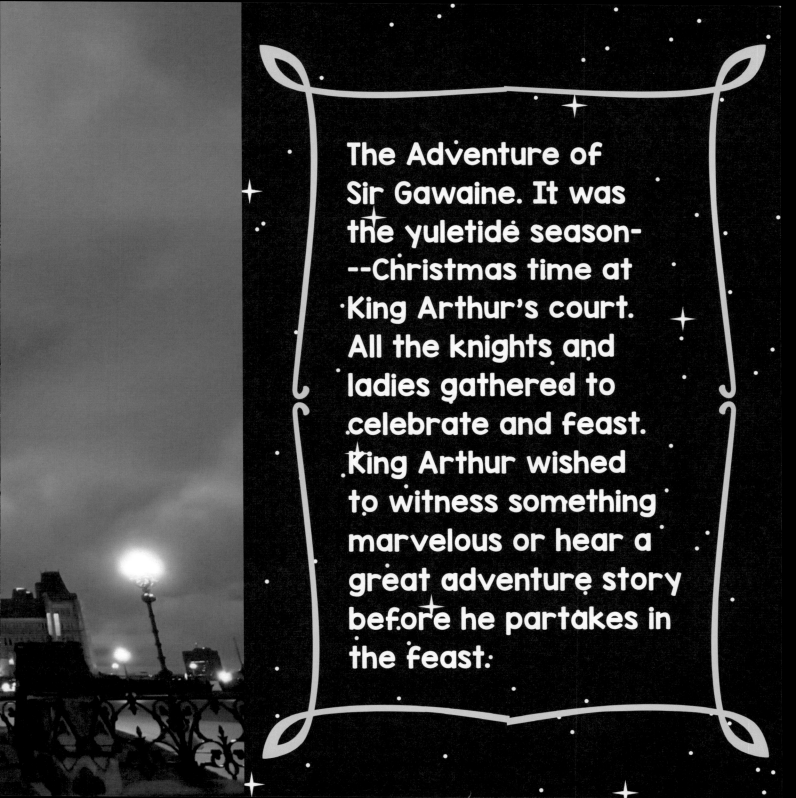

The Adventure of
Sir Gawaine. It was
the yuletide season-
--Christmas time at
King Arthur's court.
All the knights and
ladies gathered to
celebrate and feast.
King Arthur wished
to witness something
marvelous or hear a
great adventure story
before he partakes in
the feast.

Right when everyone had settled, a mysterious, gigantic stranger with emerald-green skin and clothing suddenly appeared into the hall. He rode a gigantic green horse and carried an elaborately-decorated axe.

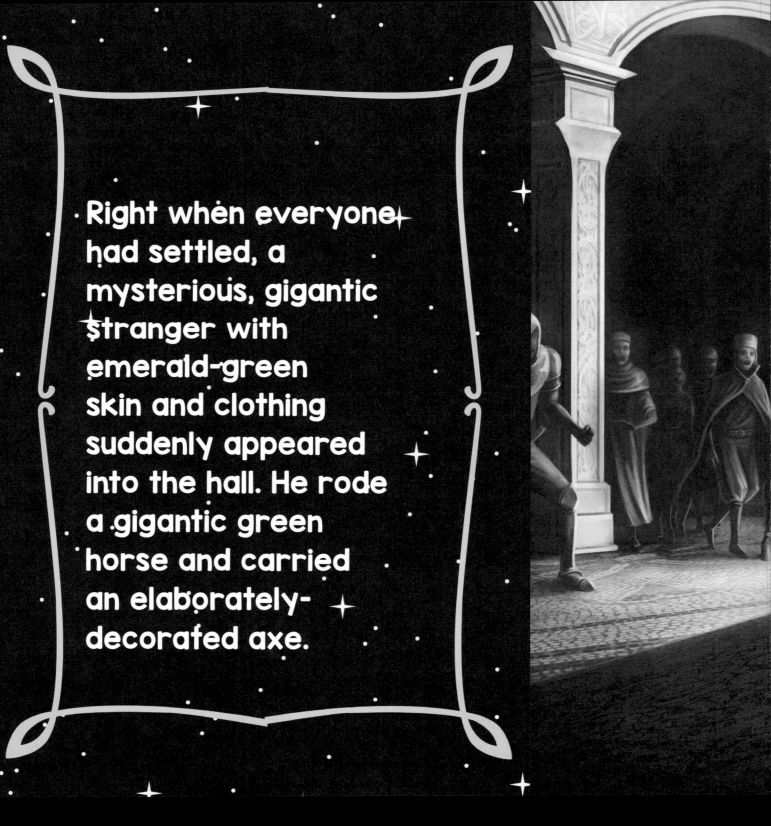

He called himself
the Green Knight. He
bellowed, saying that
he had come to test the
honor of the legendary
Knights of the Round
Table. He proposed a
game where he will
withstand a single axe
blow from anyone of the
knights.

A condition was made that a year after, the Green Knight, in turn, will do the same to the said knight. Everyone was in shock and stunned by the weirdness of the Green Knight's silly game. No one volunteered, except Sir Gawaine.

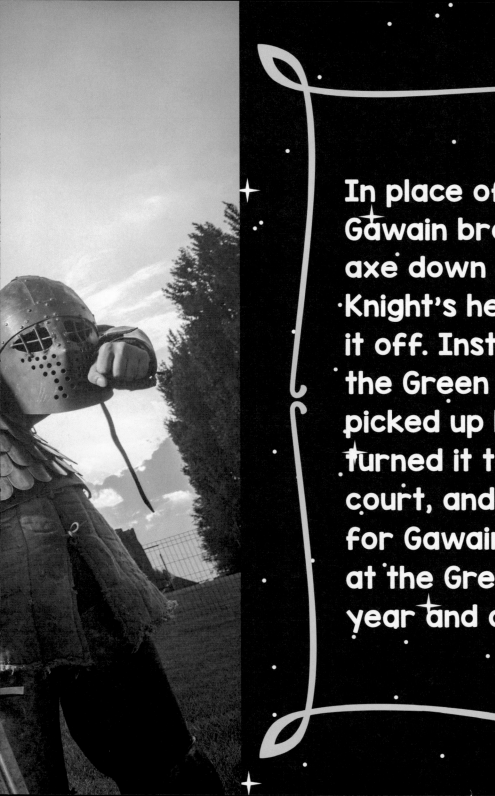

In place of the king, Gawain brought the axe down on the Green Knight's head, chopping it off. Instead of dying, the Green Knight simply picked up his own head, turned it to face the court, and announced for Gawain to meet him at the Green Chapel in a year and a day after.

Seasons passed, the day came when Sir Gawaine would do the same favor and meet with the Green Knight. Gawaine received 3 single blows of the axe but the Green Knight forgave him for his human frailties.

The Green Knight left Gawaine with only a scar and a girdle as a reminder of his very human sin of trying to covet his wife (while in disguise) and for not returning the girdle of invisibility.

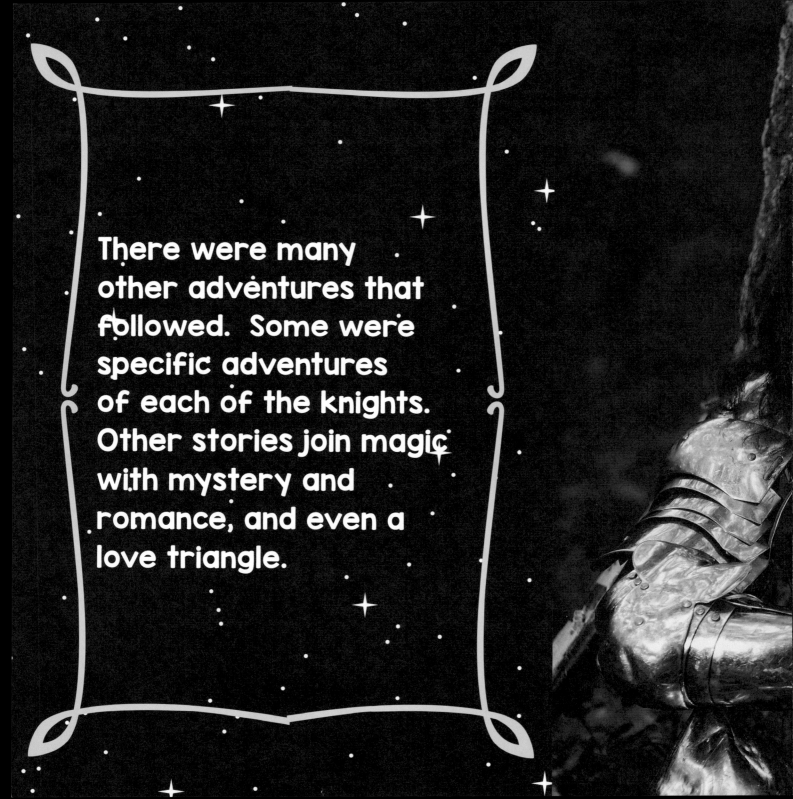

There were many other adventures that followed. Some were specific adventures of each of the knights. Other stories join magic with mystery and romance, and even a love triangle.

Truly, the tales are remarkable, enchanting, and historical.

Visit

BABY PROFESSOR
EDUCATION KIDS

www.BabyProfessorBooks.com

to download Free Baby Professor eBooks
and view our catalog of new and exciting
Children's Books